Biggest, Baddest Books

BIGGEST, BADDEST BOOK OF
FLIGHT

MARY ELIZABETH SALZMANN

Consulting Editor, Diane Craig, M.A./Reading Specialist

Super Sandcastle

An Imprint of Abdo Publishing
www.abdopublishing.com

www.abdopublishing.com

Published by Abdo Publishing, a division of ABDO, PO Box 398166, Minneapolis, Minnesota 55439. Copyright © 2015 by Abdo Consulting Group, Inc. International copyrights reserved in all countries. No part of this book may be reproduced in any form without written permission from the publisher. Super SandCastle™ is a trademark and logo of Abdo Publishing.

Printed in the United States of America, North Mankato, Minnesota
102014
012015

Editor: Liz Salzmann
Content Developer: Nancy Tuminelly
Cover and Interior Design and Production: Mighty Media, Inc.
Photo Credits: To come

Library of Congress Cataloging-in-Publication Data

Salzmann, Mary Elizabeth, 1968- author.
  Biggest, baddest book of flight / Mary Elizabeth Salzmann.
    pages cm. -- (Biggest, baddest books)
  Audience: Ages 4-9.
  ISBN 978-1-62403-515-9
  1. Aeronautics--History--Juvenile literature. I. Title. II. Title: Book of flight.
  TL547.S25 2015
  629.1309--dc23
                    2014024008

Super SandCastle™ books are created by a team of professional educators, reading specialists, and content developers around five essential components—phonemic awareness, phonics, vocabulary, text comprehension, and fluency—to assist young readers as they develop reading skills and strategies and increase their general knowledge. All books are written, reviewed, and leveled for guided reading, early reading intervention, and Accelerated Reader® programs for use in shared, guided, and independent reading and writing activities to support a balanced approach to literacy instruction.

CONTENTS

FIRST FLIGHTS

The first manned flight was in 1783. It was in a hot air balloon. Two French brothers built it.

George Cayley invented gliders. In 1853, a man flew a short distance in his glider. It was the first controlled flight.

HOT AIR BALLOON (1786)

ALBATROS II (1868)

CAYLEY'S GLIDER (1852)

Jean Marie Le Bris studied **albatrosses**. He built gliders with wings like the bird. He named them after the albatross.

Wilbur and Orville Wright lived in Ohio. They loved flight.

First they built gliders. They went to Kitty Hawk, North Carolina. They practiced flying the gliders.

Then they added an engine. They added a **propeller** to steer it. They called the plane the Wright Flyer I.

THE WRIGHT BROTHERS TESTING A GLIDER IN 1901.

THE WRIGHT STUFF

WINGS

Most airplanes have fixed wings. That means the wings don't move.

Air flows above and below the wings. The air above the wings speeds up. The air below the wings doesn't.

The different airflow speeds cause lift. The plane takes off!

LIFT

LIFT

LIFT

CROSS SECTION OF A WING

AIRFLOW

TAPERED STRAIGHT

ELLIPTICAL STRAIGHT

SWEPT BACK

TRAPEZOIDAL

DELTA

WING CONTROL

Airplane wings have flaps and spoilers. They are used during takeoff and landing.

WHAT CAN YOU SEE FROM THE WINDOW SEAT?

SPOILERS

FLAPS

FLIGHT BETWEEN THE FIRST AND SECOND WORLD WARS

Barnstorming

Barnstorming was popular after World War I. **Pilots** performed tricks with airplanes. Acrobats rode on the wings! They would go from farm to farm. That's why it was called barnstorming.

Airships

Airships don't have wings. They are filled with gas. The gas is lighter than the air outside. That causes the airship to rise. Airships were often used until about 1940. Then faster airplanes were built. Airships became less popular.

8

BREAKING THE SOUND BARRIER

WITH Chuck Yeager and the BELL X-1

Sound travels 767 miles per hour (1,234 kmh). That is 1 mile (1.6 km) in 5 seconds!

Chuck Yeager was the first **pilot** to officially fly faster than sound. He did it on October 14, 1947. The airplane was a Bell X-1.

Chuck Yeager was a fighter pilot. He fought in World War II. Then he became a test pilot for the Air Force.

HELICOPTERS

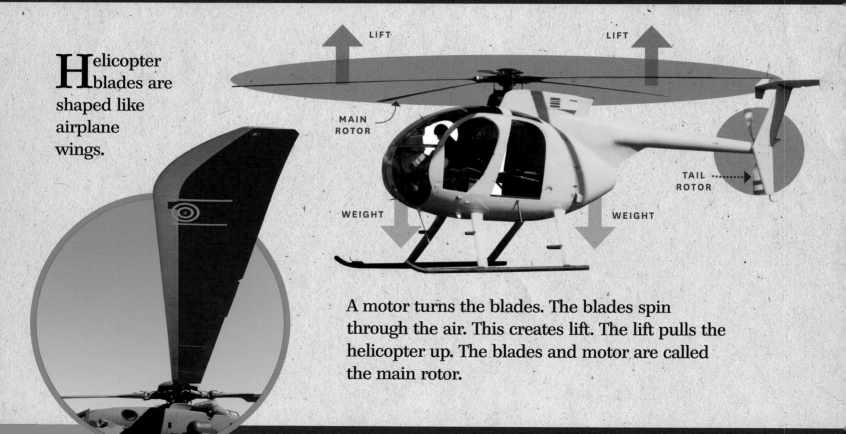

Helicopter blades are shaped like airplane wings.

LIFT

LIFT

MAIN ROTOR

TAIL ROTOR

WEIGHT

WEIGHT

A motor turns the blades. The blades spin through the air. This creates lift. The lift pulls the helicopter up. The blades and motor are called the main rotor.

TAIL ROTOR OR TWIN ROTORS?

TAIL ROTOR

Most helicopters also have a tail rotor. It is smaller than the main rotor.

TWIN ROTORS

Some helicopters have two large rotors. They spin in opposite directions.

HH-65 DOLPHIN

AH-64 APACHE

CH-47 CHINOOK

SEARCH AND RESCUE

The U.S. Coast Guard uses HH-65 Dolphin helicopters. They rescue people. They also catch criminals.

ATTACK

The AH-64 Apache is a fighter helicopter. It has a large gun and **missiles**.

HEAVY LIFT

The CH-47 Chinook is a **cargo** helicopter. It carries troops and supplies.

TITANS of the SKY

PREGNANT GUPPY

SIZE: *127 feet (39 m) long, 141-foot (43 m) wingspan*

WEIGHT: *91,000 pounds (41,275 kg)*

The Pregnant Guppy is a large **cargo** plane. The first one was built in 1962. NASA used them to move huge parts for space programs.

HOMER (MIL V-12)

SIZE: *121 feet (37 m) long, 220-foot (67 m) wingspan*

WEIGHT: *152,339 pounds (69,100 kg)*

The MIL V-12 is a Russian helicopter. It is the largest helicopter ever built. Only two of them were made.

HUGHES H-4 HERCULES "SPRUCE GOOSE"

SIZE: *219 feet (67 m) long, 321-foot (98 m) wingspan*

WEIGHT: *300,000 pounds (136,079 kg)*

The Hercules is made of wood. That's how it got the name "Spruce Goose." It has the longest **wingspan** of any aircraft. The Hercules was built to land on water. It made its only flight in 1947.

JET ENGINES

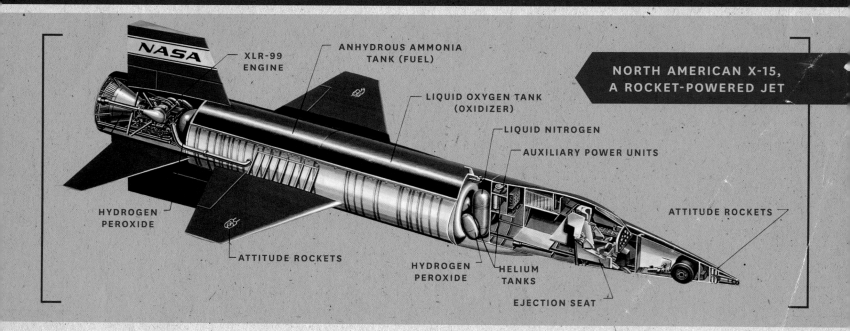

NORTH AMERICAN X-15,
A ROCKET-POWERED JET

XLR-99
ENGINE

ANHYDROUS AMMONIA
TANK (FUEL)

LIQUID OXYGEN TANK
(OXIDIZER)

LIQUID NITROGEN

AUXILIARY POWER UNITS

ATTITUDE ROCKETS

HYDROGEN
PEROXIDE

ATTITUDE ROCKETS

HYDROGEN
PEROXIDE

HELIUM
TANKS

EJECTION SEAT

A jet engine draws air in. A compressor presses the air. Fuel is added to the air. Then it is lit with an electric spark. The air shoots out the back. This pushes the plane forward.

AIRBUS A340

TURBOFAN JET ENGINES

Most large airplanes have turbofan jet engines.

TURBOFAN JET ENGINES

A turbofan jet engine has a large fan. It sucks in air. Some of the air goes into the compressor. The rest of the air flows outside it. This makes the engine quieter.

F-22 RAPTOR

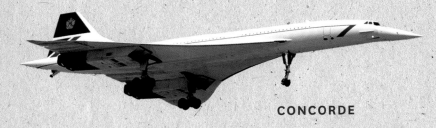

CONCORDE

TURBOJET ENGINES

A turbojet engine also takes in air. All of the air goes into the compressor. The engine is very noisy.

ROCKET ENGINES

Rocket engines don't take in air. Instead, they have chemicals inside them. The chemicals burn up. A strong jet of gas shoots out the back.

NF-104A

THE NEED FOR SPEED

THE FASTEST MANNED AIRCRAFT

528 MPH (850 KMH)

THE RARE BEAR FASTEST PROPELLER AIRCRAFT

TOP SPEED: *528 mph (850 kmh)*

DATE: *August 21, 1989*

PILOT: *Lyle Shelton*

The Grumman F8F Bearcat was a fighter plane. The fastest one was called "The Rare Bear." It was the fastest **propeller** aircraft.

SR-71 BLACKBIRD FASTEST AIR-BREATHING AIRCRAFT

TOP SPEED: *2,193 mph (3,530 kmh)*

DATE: *July 28, 1976*

PILOTS: *Captain Eldon W. Joersz and Major George T. Morgan*

The SR-71 could fly faster than a **missile**. It had a turbojet engine. It was dark blue. It was hard to see in the night sky. The color is why it was called "Blackbird."

17955

U.S. AIR FORCE

955

2,193 MPH (3,530 KMH)

4,520 MPH (7,274 KMH)

X-15 FASTEST ROCKET-POWERED AIRCRAFT

TOP SPEED: *4,520 mph (7,274 kmh)*

DATE: *October 3, 1967*

PILOT: *William "Pete" Knight*

The North American X-15 had a rocket-powered engine. It could fly to the edge of space. William Knight flew it faster than any manned airplane.

STRANGE BIRDS

VZ-9 Avrocar

The Avrocar was a secret. It was part of a U.S. military project. Two of them built in 1959. They could take off and land vertically. They looked like flying saucers.

THE FLYING PANCAKE

The Vought V-173 was built in 1942. It was called "The Flying Pancake." That was because of its shape. Only one was built. It was last flown in 1947.

THE INFLATOPLANE

Goodyear built the Inflatoplane for the U.S. Army. It was an **inflatable** airplane. Twelve of them were made. But they weren't good for military use. It was too easy to shoot them down.

TO SPACE

AND BEYOND ...

The United States had a space program. So did the Soviet Union. They both wanted to be first in space. Their rivalry was called the "Space Race."

SATURN V ROCKET (1967)

The Saturn V was a NASA rocket. It is the tallest, most powerful rocket ever flown. There were thirteen of them. They took 24 astronauts to the moon.

SATURN V LAUNCH,
MAY 20, 1969

THE SPACE SHUTTLE (1981)

NASA's Space Shuttles were reusable. They orbited the Earth. Five were built. They were *Columbia, Challenger, Discovery, Atlantis,* and *Endeavor.*

ATLANTIS WAS THE FOURTH SPACE SHUTTLE

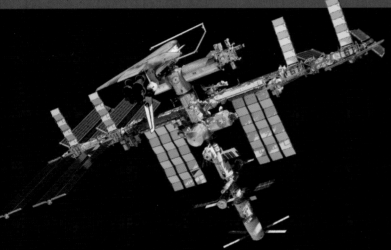

SPACESHIPTWO (2009)

SpaceShipTwo was created to give regular people rides into space. It has room for eight people. A ticket costs $200,000.

INTERNATIONAL SPACE STATION (1998)

The International Space Station is a **satellite**. It orbits the Earth. It is run by the United States, Canada, Russia, Japan, and Europe. Six people can live on it.

THE FLYING CARS OF THE FUTURE

TERRAFUGIA TF-X

The Terrafugia TF-X is an electric flying car. It can fly 500 miles (805 km) at a time. It can also be driven on roads.

AEROMOBIL

The AeroMobil is a gas-powered flying car. Its wings fold up when it's not flying. It can fly faster than 124 miles per hour (200 kmh). It can drive 100 miles per hour (160 kmh).

WHAT DO YOU KNOW ABOUT FLIGHT?

1. AIRPLANE WINGS HAVE FLAPS AND SPOILERS. **TRUE OR FALSE?**

2. AIRSHIPS HAVE WINGS. **TRUE OR FALSE?**

3. HELICOPTER BLADES ARE NOT SHAPED LIKE AIRPLANE WINGS. **TRUE OR FALSE?**

4. ROCKET ENGINES DON'T TAKE IN AIR. **TRUE OR FALSE?**

ANSWERS: 1) TRUE 2) FALSE 3) FALSE 4) TRUE

23

ALBATROSS – a large seabird.

CARGO – goods carried on a ship, plane, or other vehicle.

INFLATABLE – able to be filled with air or another gas.

MISSILE – a large weapon that can be shot at a target.

PILOT – a person who operates an aircraft or a ship.

PROPELLER – a device with turning blades used to move a vehicle such as an airplane or a boat.

SATELLITE – a manufactured object that orbits the earth.

WINGSPAN – the distance from one wing tip to the other.